THE AMERICAN
INDIANS

PONY TRACKS

WEATHER CLEAR

MOUNTAIN PEAKS CROSSED

RED TOMAHAWK SHOWS
THAT FOUR TEPEES
WERE ATTACKED

RIVER CROSSED

PARTY AWAY TWO MOONS (MONTH

INDIAN BUFFALO-HIDE PAINTING:

SIOUX WAR PARTY ATTACKING A CROW CAMP

The Plains Indians recorded in picture writing important events in their tribal history. Only victories were noted — never defeats.

The record shown here is taken from an actual Indian painting and tells how a band of six Sioux braves successfully attacked an enemy camp; that they crossed three mountain peaks and crossed a river on their return, and that the weather was clear during the two months (moons) they were away.

For further information about picture writing, see the page titled "The Painted Tepee."

THE AMERICAN
INDIANS

The Big Book of Indians

By SYDNEY E. FLETCHER

GROSSET & DUNLAP • Publishers • NEW YORK

WAR DANCE · An Indian rarely went to war or started out on a dangerous mission without first appealing to his personal "Medicine" for protection from evil spirits. His "Medicine" may have been a good luck charm, a sacred object, or an amulet of traditional tribal importance. There were also various semi-religious ceremonies, each with its own set of songs and dance rituals. A band of warriors about to go

on the warpath gathered in the evening to dance the War Dance, to sing and to practice religious rites to insure the defeat of their enemy. If the warriors returned in triumph, the braves presented to the women of their families the scalps taken from the enemy. Then they held a great feast and danced the Scalp Dance with songs and cheers celebrating the victory.

BUFFALO HUNT · Ranging over the prairies in countless numbers, the buffalo provided the Plains Tribes not only with food but also clothing, utensils and shelter. Buffalo meat, cut into thin strips, was dried in the sun. Then it was stored in rawhide cases to be used for food in the winter. Buffalo hide was made into moccasins, ropes, shields, snowshoes and tent covers. Pelts taken in the winter, when

the buffalo's hair was long, were used for bedding, and for clothes of extra weight and warmth. The sinews furnished bowstrings and thread for sewing. The horns were made into spoons and drinking cups. Buffalo hoofs furnished glue for mending. In fact, to many Indian tribes, the buffalo symbolized their very existence, and was considered the greatest gift that could have been bestowed upon them.

KACHINA DOLLS · The Indians of the Southwest held many religious ceremonies for the purpose of bringing rain, increasing the harvest and praying for good hunting. The Indians believed that the "Kachinas" (Kuh-*chee*-nuhs) took part in these prayer festivals. The Kachinas were mythical beings who, the Indians thought, visited their vil-

lages on very special occasions. They were represented by dancers masked and painted like the tribe's picture of each Kachina. Small, carved cottonwood dolls, painted and decorated with feathers, also were symbols of the Kachinas' presence. After the ceremony, the dolls were given to the children to play with.

OTTER TEPEE   SNOW TEPEE   CROW TEPEE   SNAKE TEPEE

THE PAINTED TEPEE · The Plains Tribes, following the buffalo herds, lived a nomadic life, moving from place to place. Each family lived in a tepee of buffalo hides sewn together with thread made from the sinews of buffaloes. The tepees were painted with brightly colored decorations. The band at the top was a picture of the sky at night, showing the Big Dipper or the Indian emblem of the Morning

YELLOW BUFFALO TEPEE   BIG ROCK TEPEE

Star, the Maltese cross. In the center, the owner painted the religious design of his family, or else a symbol of an important event in his tribal history. The band at the bottom was supposed to be the earth. The peaked upper edge stood for rounded ridges or sharp mountains. The discs inside the band were "dusty stars," the name the Indians gave to the puffballs growing in clusters on the plains.

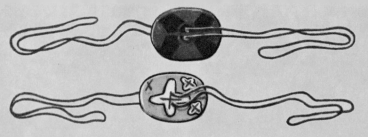

BUZZER · Two holes were made in a disc of hard clay or a circular piece of wood, and a cord was passed through the holes. The ends were tied to form a loop on each side. The loops were held, one in each hand, and the cord was twisted. When the disc was spun it made a humming sound as the ends of the cord were pulled and relaxed.

RING AND DART · A ring of wrapped corn-husk, four inches in diameter, was placed on the ground ten feet away from the players. Each player had two darts which he threw, trying to hit the center of the ring. The child whose dart hit closest to the center of the ring won all the other children's darts.

SHINNY · A post was set at each end of the ballground to serve as a goal. With a stick like our hockey stick, the player smacked a ball made of tightly wrapped deer hair covered with buckskin. To score, the ball had to hit one of the goalposts.

TOSSING THE STICK · Played by I dian children of the Southwest, th game started as part of the very ol religious Flute Ceremony. Two gir each threw a small ring, or "annulet

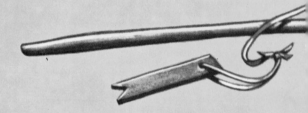

BULL-ROARER · Used ceremonially b some tribes, the "whizzer" also was boy's toy. A thin, flat, rectangula piece of wood, one- and one-half by s inches, with a notch cut at one en

WHIP TOP · A twirl of the finge started the top spinning. It was ke whirling by quickly hitting its low point with the whip. One game w played by marking out a small squa on the ground with a small opening c

INDIAN CHILDREN'S TOYS AND GAMES

SNOW-SNAKE · A narrow, shallow rut was made in the snow by dragging a log over the surface. Then a "snake" was held length-wise above the rut, and the player, with short, quick steps, threw the "snake" along the rut. The children were divided into two sides, and the side whose "snakes" ran farthest won the game.

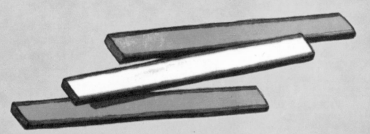

STICK DICE · The players were divided into two sides. Three sticks were painted red on one side white on the other. The first player threw the sticks rapidly on the ground. He scored them as they fell. Three white sides up counted ten points; three reds up counted five; two reds and one white counted three; two whites and one red up counted two. The side scoring the most points won.

nd a boy threw a cylinder, from one cloud-terrace" into another. These atterns, which the priests traced on e ground with colored corn meal, re-mbled our game of hopscotch.

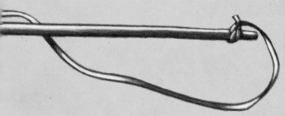

as attached by a hide thong a yard ng to the end of a stick. The boy then hirled the stick around his head, aking the flat piece of wood flutter pidly with a loud whizzing noise.

JUMPING TOAD · The object of this game was to hit either end of the wooden tipcat sharply with the buckskin ball attached to the stick. This sent the tipcat up in the air. The player who missed forfeited his stake.

ach side. Each player started his top pinning on the ground outside the quare. Then he tried to drive the top rough one of the four openings with e whip while the top was spinning. he first top in was the winner.

SHOOT-ARROW · The players stood in a circle. A boy ran around the outside of the circle, dragging a bundle of rags on a string. The players each put up one arrow as a stake, then shot at the bundle as it went past. The first child to hit it won all the arrows.

COVERED WAGON ATTACK · When the Western frontier was opened, many pioneer families began crossing the plains in covered wagons. They killed the game and drove buffalo herds from the regions through which they passed. The Plains Tribes, angry at the invasion of their hunting grounds, went on the warpath. They attacked wagon trains and sometimes massacred entire parties. Usually, ad-

vance scouts gave warning in time for the settlers to swing the big "prairie schooners" out of line and place them end to end to form a circular barricade. Teams of horses and yokes of oxen were brought inside the barricade. Then, while hardy pioneer women tended the wounded and loaded guns, the men fought off the Indians. Many a wagon train was saved in this way.

RUNNING OFF HORSES · The most important possession of the Plains Indian was his horse. Without his horse he would have been helpless, both in hunting buffalo and in making war. For this reason, the horses of a village were carefully guarded at night. The best buffalo-running and war ponies were tethered close to their owners' tepees. But every once in a while, a few bold young braves from

another tribe would succeed in making their way unseen into an enemy camp. They would cut the picket ropes of six or eight horses. Then each brave would leap on the back of a horse and, riding bareback, run the rest off under the very noses of the guards. This was considered an outstanding act of bravery, because the young braves knew that if they were caught, they would be put to death.

ON THE MOVE · The Plains Tribes used a horse litter, called a "travois," when they changed camps. The smaller ends of two tepee poles were fastened to a pony's sides, crossing above its head, with the larger ends dragging behind on the ground. A crossframe and a network of rawhide strips placed on the poles formed a kind of sled. On this, young children, the aged and the sick could be carried, as

well as camp equipment, such as tepee covers, as shown here. Sometimes a canopy of bent branches covered with animal skins was used for protection against the sun and rain. Babies traveled in their cradles on their mothers' backs. The women also carried the men's shields and Medicine bags. A big camp could be taken down or put up with unbelievable speed.

GRIZZLY BEAR HUNT · Before a young Indian could be considered a warrior, he had to perform a brave deed. The bravest deed he could perform to prove his fearlessness was to kill a ferocious grizzly bear. When the young brave had tracked down a grizzly bear, he apologized to the bear for attacking it, and explained that he was doing it only because it was necessary. Of course the bear didn't under-

stand him, but this was all part of the ceremony. After he killed the bear, the brave took it home, and the tribe brought gifts to the dead bear. The Indians believed that the mythical chief of all bears would then hear that Indians were very kind to bears. Later, the Indian removed the long claws of his grizzly bear and made them into a necklace, which became his most prized possession.

TOTEM POLES AND CANOES · The totem poles shown here were carved out of giant cedar logs. Symbols of family pride and position, totem poles, in a way, told a picture history of the particular households before which they stood. After the carving was completed, they were painted and put in the ground as memorials to dead

leaders. Similar to the totem crests and legends are the decorations on the prow of the ceremonial canoe shown here. The Northwest Coast Indians traveled almost entirely by water. Their canoes varied in size from small ones, carrying two or three men, to sea-going war canoes sixty feet long, which carried up to sixty men.

EQUIPMENT AND IMPLEMENTS
USED BY VARIOUS INDIAN TRIBES

Descriptions of the articles shown on these pages will be found immediately following.

HEADDRESS

BOWL

CEREMONIAL WAND

SHIELD

BEAVER TRAP

POLES

EARS

FLAPS

PINS

OUTSIDE POLES

COV

QUIRT AND RATTLE

PEGS

PLAINS TEPEE

ENTR COV

PORCUPINE QUILL MOCCASIN

BEADED MOCCASINS

PARFLÊCHE

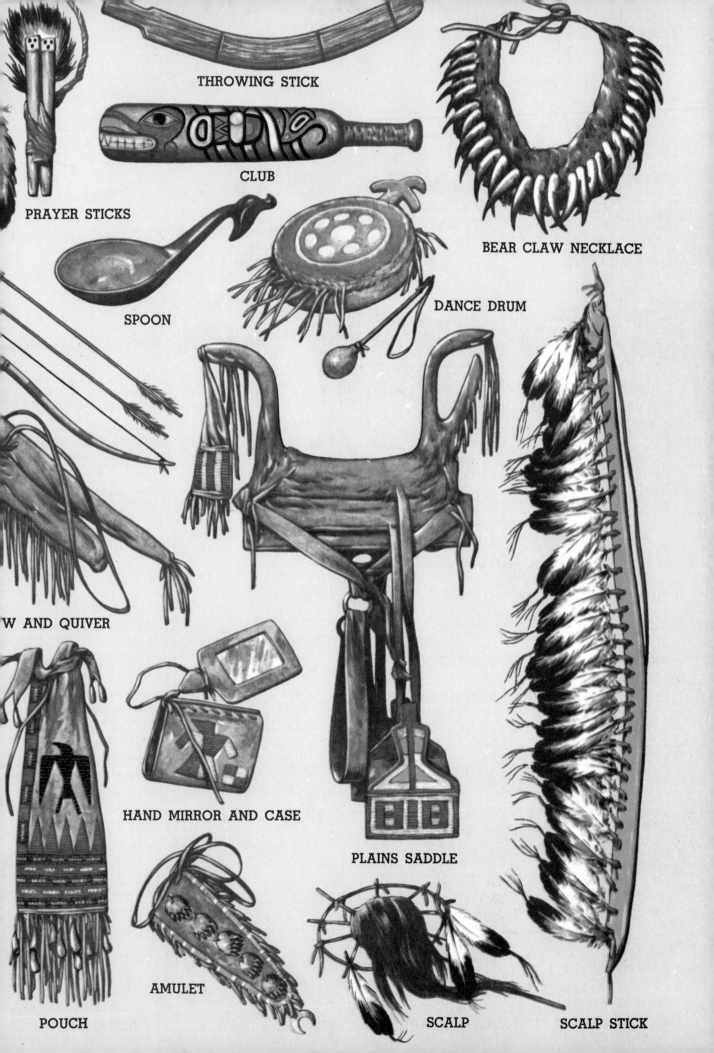

THROWING STICK

CLUB

PRAYER STICKS

BEAR CLAW NECKLACE

SPOON

DANCE DRUM

W AND QUIVER

HAND MIRROR AND CASE

PLAINS SADDLE

POUCH

AMULET

SCALP

SCALP STICK

INDIAN DRAWING
OF TWO CROW WARRIORS

A DESCRIPTIVE DICTIONARY OF INDIAN IMPLEMENTS AND EQUIPMENT

AMULET (Sauk). Decorated with mole paws and a beaded border, this good luck charm was worn around the neck to ward off evil spirits.

BEAR CLAW NECKLACE (Cree). One of the most valued insignia of a warrior, the necklace was made of grizzly bear claws three or four inches long, on a foundation of otter skin.

BEAVER TRAP (Ojibwa). This trap had no teeth to mar the beaver pelt, nor was any bait used. Instead, the trap was set under water, where the unwary beaver who blundered into it drowned.

BIRCH BARK CANOE (Winnebago). The Indian trapper and his son, shown on the title page, made their canoe of "canoe birch," that is, a tree trunk clean of branches and fairly free of knots. Girdling the tree, the Indians pried the bark off in six-foot slabs. This was done in the spring when the sap had started running and the bark could be removed easily. The ribs, made of spruce, were soaked in water until they were pliable, then bent to shape and fitted to the spruce keel. The complete framework, consisting of keel, stem and stern pieces, ribs and inner gunwales, was inverted. Then the birch bark sheets, also water-soaked until pliable, were laced in place with spruce root fiber. Finally the outer gunwales were added, all seams were cemented watertight with native spruce gum, and the trappers had a sturdy hunting canoe measuring eighteen feet in length.

BOW AND QUIVER (Navaho). The sinew-backed bow was strengthened by gluing on animal sinew. The quiver was made of buckskin. The top-shaped arrowhead was used to stun small game. For big game and war, the sharp-pointed arrow was used.

BOWL (Zuñi). Household storage, cooking and serving vessels were mostly of clay, modeled to the desired size and shape and dried in the sun. The designs were painted on with a brush of yucca fiber or a sharp stick. Next, the vessels were placed bottom side up on small stones and covered with fuel. A continuous heat was maintained until the vessels were fired.

CEREMONIAL WAND (Sioux). Two buffalo horns forming a "banner stone" symbolized the importance of the buffalo in Indian life. The beaded handle and horsehair ends were decorations.

CLUB (Tlingit). Used in killing seals and salmon, the decorations represented a killer whale with dorsal fin bent down. The Northwest Coast Indians believed that all fish, birds, and land and sea mammals possessed varying degrees of supernatural power. The killer whale was thought to be the greatest of all living animals. The Indians believed he lived in a village under the sea, his body being the canoe in which he traveled.

DANCE DRUM (Arapaho). The dance drum was made by stretching a piece of green, or "wet," rawhide over each side of a section, or "hoop," cut from a hollow tree. The head of the drumstick was usually filled with gravel.

HAND MIRROR AND CASE (Sioux). A small hand mirror, fitted with a buckskin case and decorated in a beaded Thunderbird design, was used by warriors when painting their faces and other bare parts of their bodies. On the warpath, they wore red and dark blue paint for protection and as a symbol of success. Black was worn by the victorious warriors in the scalp dance.

HEADDRESS (Crow). The war headdress was of horsehair mounted on a frame of stiff hide shaped to the head and tied under the chin with buckskin thongs. The warrior called it his "enemy bonnet," and wore it only when on the warpath. Eagle feathers on a war bonnet were a badge of honor reserved only for great leaders.

MOCCASINS (Blackfoot). Moccasins with porcupine quill embroidery were traditional with the Plains Tribes. The quills were softened with water, then flattened and dyed, leaving them with a smooth, glossy, strawlike surface. Colored glass beads were imported from Europe about 1800.

PARFLÊCHE (Shoshoni). The parflêche, or packing case, of the nomadic Plains Indians was made of a piece of rawhide, the sides and ends of which were folded together and laced with buckskin thongs. The designs in earth colors were painted on by Indian women.

PLAINS SADDLE (Arapaho). The frame was made of wood or elkhorn covered with fresh buffalo hide which shrunk tight as it dried. During the drying, the saddle frame was pegged down to the ground. The very high pommel and crupper, typical of the Plains Tribes, can be traced back to ancient Asia. A hook was put under the pommel to carry the rope. Stirrups also were made of wood bound with rawhide. The Indian bridle was a simple rope or thong looped around the horse's jaw.

PLAINS TEPEE (Kiowa). The cone-shaped tepee was constructed of about twenty poles set up in a circle and inclined together at the top. The outside poles attached to the smoke flaps, or "ears," controlled the size of the smoke hole and the upward draft of the fire inside. The poles were covered with as many as twenty-four buffalo skins. Adjustable to any climate, the tepee could be taken down quickly and transported to another place.

POUCH (Sioux). The tobacco pouch and pipe case were made of smoke-tanned buckskin and decorated with the design of the Thunderbird, the mythological Indian bird.

PRAYER STICKS (Hopi). Notched and colored, these were offered during the rain ceremony to the gods who dwelt in the six sacred springs, that they might urge the cloud people to sprinkle the parched earth with rain.

QUIRT AND RATTLE (Cheyenne). The Cheyenne Dog Soldier's quirt and rattle were his badge of authority. The Dog Soldiers were a band of young braves assigned to police the camp circle, keep order on the march and on the buffalo hunt, enforce the orders of the chief, and punish violators. The handle of a quirt like the one shown was studded with brass tacks. The rattle was made of a dried gourd covered with buckskin, and the wrapped handle was decorated with horsehair. Pebbles placed inside completed the rattle.

SCALP AND SCALP STICK (Assiniboin). Many of the Plains Tribes believed that scalping an enemy destroyed his soul, thus eliminating him as a future foe. The scalp was stretched to dry on a willow hoop, but was kept only until after the victory celebration. It was then carefully buried, and an eagle feather attached to the Scalp Stick took its place for trophy purposes.

SHIELD (Kiowa). The shield of the mounted warrior was made of thick bull-buffalo hide. Carried on the left arm by a belt passing over the shoulder, so the warrior's left hand would be free to grasp the bow, the shield could stop an arrow or turn the stroke of a lance.

SPOON (Seneca). This carved cooking utensil with a bird handle is a good example of the handicraft of the Seneca Indians, one of the five tribes that formed the powerful Iroquois Confederacy.

THROWING STICK (Zuñi). The throwing stick of the Southwestern Indian was used to hunt small game. Unlike the Australian boomerang, it did not return to the thrower.

WAR CANOE (Haida). Hollowed out of a cedar log, the projecting bow and high stern were for travel in heavy ocean waters.

MODEL OF HAIDA WAR CANOE

PONY TRACKS

WEATHER CLEAR

MOUNTAIN PEAKS CROSSED

RED TOMAHAWK SHOWS
THAT FOUR TEPEES
WERE ATTACKED

RIVER CROSSED

PARTY AWAY TWO MOONS (MONTI

INDIAN BUFFALO-HIDE PAINTING:

SIOUX WAR PARTY ATTACKING A CROW CAMP

The Plains Indians recorded in picture writing important events in their tribal history. Only victories were noted — never defeats.

The record shown here is taken from an actual Indian painting and tells how a band of six Sioux braves successfully attacked an enemy camp; that they crossed three mountain peaks and crossed a river on their return, and that the weather was clear during the two months (moons) they were away.

For further information about picture writing, see the page titled "The Painted Tepee."